I Love
HUGS

We all love hugs, and lots of animals love hugs too!

When you give a hug, you get one right back.

That's why hugging makes cuddly creatures feel safe, relaxed, warm, and happy.

We love to hold each other **tight**. We play fight and then we **hug** to show we are still **friends**.

Baby elephants love to play. They pretend to fight and enjoy the rough-and-tumble of playtime.

This is my dad's big belly hug! I love his warm and cozy cuddles.

Emperor penguins live near the South Pole and have to survive snow, ice, and freezing winds. A chick sits on its father's feet. His fluffy belly acts like a blanket to keep the chick warm.

I love to **hug.**
I feel safe
when I hug
my **mom.**
I know she will
look after **me.**

When a lemur baby is born it holds
on to its mother's belly. As the
baby gets stronger, it can hold
on to its mother's back when
she leaps between trees.

The best hugs are big bear hugs.

A polar bear mother normally has two cubs at a time, and she will fight to protect them. The cubs play together to exercise, and to learn how to hunt.

We love to **cuddle** at bedtime. It's easy to fall **asleep** when you know someone loves **YOU.**

Sea otters spend most of their lives at sea, and they often hold hands when they sleep. Baby otters are called pups and their mothers hold them on their tummies.

When your friends are feeling sad, just wrap your arms around them and gently squeeze.

Gibbons have very long arms. They use them to swing through the trees, and can travel 30 feet (9 m) in just one swing. Their long arms are also perfect for giving comforting hugs.

The world isn't so scary when you've got someone to hug.

Meerkats live in groups of 20 or more called clans. They live underground in burrows but come up to the surface to look for food. Meerkats stand guard near their burrows and look out for danger.

We love to hug trees! We are brothers, and holding hands makes us feel all warm inside.

Mother raccoons have babies once a year. They have three to seven babies at a time, and they look after them in dens they have built in trees.

My dad gives me cuddles. It's his way of showing me just how much he cares.

A father lion looks after his cubs when the mother goes hunting. The cubs often pester their dad, but he gently pushes them away if they get too annoying!

We love to **snuggle** up.

We call this hug a

buddy body blanket!

It is often cold and snowy in the places where Japanese macaques live. They keep warm by bathing in natural hot water springs, and by cuddling!

I know my mom loves me because she wraps her arms around me tells me so.

Chimps are our closest relatives, so it is no wonder they like to hug as much as we do. They also like to play, and to be tickled and kissed!

Mom's asleep, but I can still sneak in for a quick snuggle...

Taking care of newborn tiger cubs is hard work! Cubs are born blind, so their mother must do everything for them. Tiger cubs begin to hunt when they are six months old.

We love a group hug! Everyone can join in...

Orangutan babies stay with their mother until they are about ten years old. Baby orangutans love to play, hold hands, hug, and kiss.

A hug is worth thousand words. We don't need to talk when we hold each other tight.

When newborn pandas are born
they are as tiny as an apple.
A cub feeds on its mother's milk
to grow. Later it will learn how
to find and eat bamboo.

Here are three good reasons for hugging.

A cuddle is a good way to show someone you love them.

♥

A snuggle makes you feel safe and warm

♥

A hug is worth a thousand words...

Can you think of any more?

Editor: Tasha Percy
Designer: Natalie Godwin

Copyright © QEB Publishing 2015

First published in the United States in 2015 by
QEB Publishing
3 Wrigley, Suite A
Irvine, CA 92618

www.qed-publishing.co.uk

A CIP record for this book is available from the Library of Congress.

ISBN 978 1 60992 719 6

Printed in China